Hello, Family Members,

Learning to read is one of the most important accomplishments of early childhood. **Hello Reader!** books are designed to help children become skilled readers who like to read. Beginning readers learn to read by remembering frequently used words like "the," "is," and "and"; by using phonics skills to decode new words; and by interpreting picture and text clues. These books provide both the stories children enjoy and the structure they need to read fluently and independently. Here are suggestions for helping your child *before*, *during*, and *after* reading:

Before
- Look at the cover and pictures and have your child predict what the story is about.
- Read the story to your child.
- Encourage your child to chime in with familiar words and phrases.
- Echo read with your child by reading a line first and having your child read it after you do.

During
- Have your child think about a word he or she does not recognize right away. Provide hints such as "Let's see if we know the sounds" and "Have we read other words like this one?"
- Encourage your child to use phonics skills to sound out new words.
- Provide the word for your child when more assistance is needed so that he or she does not struggle and the experience of reading with you is a positive one.
- Encourage your child to have fun by reading with a lot of expression . . . like an actor!

After
- Have your child keep lists of interesting and favorite words.
- Encourage your child to read the books over and over again. Have him or her read to brothers, sisters, grandparents, and even teddy bears. Repeated readings develop confidence in young readers.
- Talk about the stories. Ask and answer questions. Share ideas about the funniest and most interesting characters and events in the stories.

I do hope that you and your child enjoy this book.

—Francie Alexander
Reading Specialist,
Scholastic's Learning Ventures

*Dedicated to the memory of my beloved mother Carrie Sherman
and my dear son Damon Jackson
—G.J.*

*For Aldous and Ernest
—C.V.W. and Y-H.H.*

Text copyright © 2000 by Garnet Jackson.
Illustrations copyright © 2000 by Cornelius Van Wright.
All rights reserved. Published by Scholastic Inc.
SCHOLASTIC, HELLO READER, CARTWHEEL BOOKS and associated logos
are trademarks and/or registered trademarks of Scholastic Inc.

Library of Congress Cataloging-in-Publication Data
Jackson, Garnet.
    George Washington / by Garnet Jackson; illustrated by Cornelius Van Wright
and Ying-Hwa Hu.
        p.   cm. — (Hello reader! Level 2)
    "Cartwheel books."
    Summary: A simple biography of George Washington, the first president of the
United States.
    ISBN 0-439-09867-X
    1. Washington, George, 1732-1799 Juvenile literature.
2. Presidents — United States Biography Juvenile literature.
[1. Washington, George, 1732-1799. 2 Presidents.]   I. Van Wright, Cornelius, ill.
II. Hu, Ying-Hwa, ill.   III. Title.   IV. Series.
E312.66.J29   2000
973.4'092—dc21
[B]

99-15261
CIP

12 11 10 9 8 7 6 5 4 3 2 1   00 01 02 03 04

Printed in the U.S.A.   24
First Printing, February 2000

George Washington

by Garnet Jackson

Illustrated by Cornelius Van Wright and Ying-Hwa Hu

Hello Reader! — Level 2

SCHOLASTIC INC. Cartwheel ·B·O·O·K·S· ®

New York   Toronto   London   Auckland   Sydney
Mexico City   New Delhi   Hong Kong

It was a cold winter morning on February 22, 1732. This was more than 200 years ago.

Inside a Virginia farmhouse where it was warm and cozy, a special baby boy was born. The baby's name was George Washington.

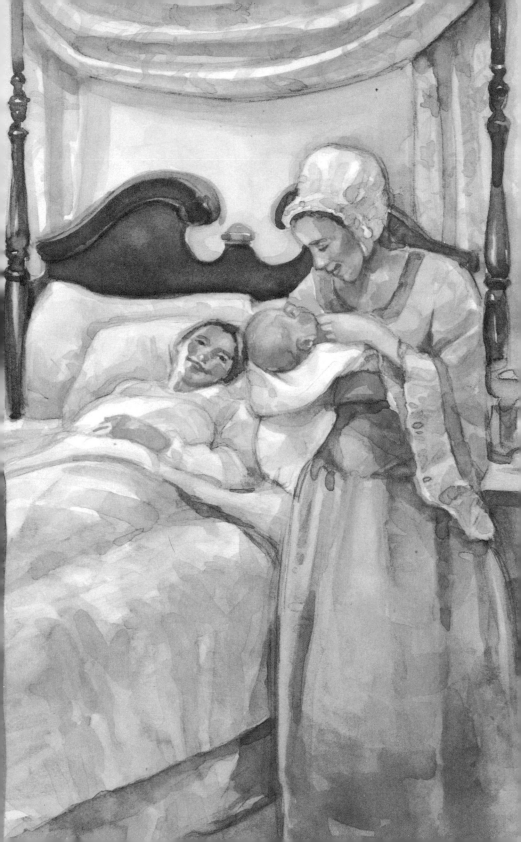

As little George grew up, he loved
the farm and all of the animals.
He loved his horse best of all.

George had two older brothers who lived away. He lived with a younger sister and three younger brothers. They followed George's every move.

"Let's play *Follow the Leader*," said Betty.

"George is the leader," said John.

Samuel and Charles agreed.

George went to a small country school. He worked very hard. He was one of the smartest students. George was also the most honest boy in school.

He grew up very fast. He was bigger
and taller than all of the other boys.
Everyone looked up to George.
Sometimes George would choose games
for his classmates to play.
"George is a natural-born leader," his
schoolmaster would say.

In school George liked to read and to write. He liked numbers. But he liked to make maps and measure land best of all. This is called surveying.

George practiced by measuring the
vegetable gardens on his farm.

Many farmers wanted George to survey their land. It would help them to know how much seed to buy when it was time to plant their crops.

George was only a boy of sixteen. But the farmers trusted him. They knew George was very smart and honest. "He will do a perfect job," one farmer said to another.

George's big brother, Lawrence, took him on a surveying trip in the Virginia wilderness. They stayed many cold and rainy days and nights. There were many wild animals. George learned how to take care of himself in the woods.

Living in the wilderness helped George to become an even greater leader. When he was only twenty years old he became a major in the Virginia army.

In 1754 a war broke out. French settlers and Native Americans in the Ohio Valley would not let the English settlers have farms there.

George Washington was called to help the English settlers. He was now Colonel Washington. He led the English soldiers and they won the war. Everyone looked up to Colonel Washington.

One day, George met a lovely lady named Martha Custis. She was a widow with two children. They fell in love and were married in 1759.

George and Martha Washington moved
into a beautiful mansion in Mount
Vernon, Virginia. They had many parties,
laughter, and fun in their home.

But Colonel Washington was soon called to war again. It was 1775. America was a very small country with only thirteen colonies then. During this time England ruled America. The rulers in England were mistreating America. They wanted America to pay unfair taxes.

A war broke out. The Americans chose
George Washington as their leader.

The war lasted eight years. The Colonel was now General George Washington. Through his leadership, the American colonies won the war. America was no longer ruled by England. The colonies became the United States of America.

Americans were very happy. But the
new little country needed a leader.
Everyone in the land wanted one and
only one man for this job—General
George Washington. So they made him
the first president of the United States
of America on April 30, 1789.

On the day of his inauguration, President George Washington rode on a beautiful white horse on his way to the ceremony.

"Hooray!" people cheered when President
Washington stood before them to give his
speech. Some people cried with joy.

President Washington was a great president. He traveled all over America to see what the country needed. He passed good laws to help America.

George Washington was president for eight years. Afterwards, he went back to his home in Mount Vernon. He enjoyed good times and laughter again with Martha, his family, and friends.

Americans will never forget the first president of their land.